The art of the garden

Designed by Gillian Greenwood

Miles Hadfield

The art
of the garden

a dutton vista pictureback
General editor David Herbert

Set in 9 pt Plantin, 2 pts leaded
Published in London by Studio Vista Limited
Blue Star House, Highgate Hill, N19
and in New York by E. P. Dutton and Co Inc
201 Park Avenue South, New York 3 NY
Made and printed in Great Britain by
Richard Clay (The Chaucer Press), Ltd, Bungay, Suffolk

Contents

Introduction

For many centuries man has, by combining the functions of architecture, horticulture, arboriculture, human sweat and toil (lately replaced by the internal-combustion engine), produced or attempted to produce his worldly paradises. Sometimes they are for his own private enjoyment—secret places in which to hide from the world and its follies. At other times (usually when he happens to be an emperor) they form the permanent scenery for aggrandizement, parade and display. In the former category is the garden that the quiet poet Shenstone made at the Leasowes; in the latter, examples range from the hanging gardens of Babylon, made to please a Persian lady, to the magnificence of Versailles, designed to display the Sun King, Louis XIV, in an appropriate setting.

These are but two types of garden; there are indeed as many different kinds as there are gardeners, but there is one distinction that divides them all into two broad classes: those that are contrived in whatever manner by artists, and those that are humdrum, unimaginative works—as often as not made with no higher objective than to follow some fashion.

Here we shall try to concern ourselves with the former. Taste being fallible and changeable, and the definition of art equally so, we can do no more than offer a very limited selection of representative types. We have tried to classify these by means of the ideals or outlook that inspired them. Little attempt has been made to treat the subject historically; origins are scarcely mentioned. Plans and construction are not our concern; our aim is to make a photographic survey of gardens as they are today, gardens which appear to us to have been designed with something more than horticultural or architectural craft. Our selection is limited geographically. The gardens of India or other tropical countries are scarcely mentioned. We are, too, firmly rooted to the past and the present; such pointers as look to the future seem to us to be tentative and inconclusive, and it is difficult at present to find any consistent aesthetic forward trend. At times one feels despairingly that tomorrow's gardens may be no more than a sterilized, labour-saving paradise for commercial plant-breeders, where art and craft are replaced by mechanical gadgets.

But in the meantime, we can look at and, above all, enjoy many of the great gardens of yesterday which have survived until today.

The inspiration of architecture

The Villa Lante near Viterbo (below) dates from about 1570. It gives us a clue to the elements of the Italian Renaissance garden, the essential qualities of which are defined in Alberti's *Ten Books of Architecture*, published in 1485. After describing the 'delicacies' of the villa, Alberti writes: '. . . we must add those of well-disposed

Gardens and beautiful Trees, together with Porticoes in the Garden, where you may enjoy either Sun or Shade. To these add some little pleasant Meadow, with fine Springs of Water bursting out in different Places where least expected. Let the Walks be terminated by Trees that enjoy a perpetual Verdure, and particularly on that Side which is best sheltered from Winds, let them be enclosed with Box, which is presently injured and rotted by strong Winds, and especially by the least Spray from the Sea. In open Places, most exposed to the Sun, some set Myrtles, which will flourish extremely in the Summer: But Theophrastus affirms that the Myrtle, the Laurel, and the Ivy rejoyce in the Shade, and therefore directs us to plant them thick, that they may mutually shelter one another from the Sun by their own Shade: Nor let there be wanting Cypress-trees cloathed with Ivy. Let the Ground also be here and there thrown into those Figures that are most commended in the Platforms of Houses, Circles, Semicircles, and the like, then surrounded with Laurels, Cedars, Junipers with their Branches intermixed and twining one into the other. Phiteon of Agrigentum, though but a private Man, had in his House three hundred Vases of Stone, each whereof would hold an hundred Amphoras, or about fifteen of our Hogsheads. Such Vases are very fine Ornaments for Fountains in Gardens. The Ancients used to make their Walks into a Kind of Arbours by Means of Vines supported by Columns of Marble of the Corinthian Order, which were ten of their own Diameter in Height. The Trees ought to be planted in Rows exactly even, and answering to one another exactly upon straight Lines: and the Gardens should be enriched with rare Plants, and such are in most Esteem among the Physicians. It was a good agreeable Piece of Flattery among the ancient Gardeners, to trace their Masters' Names in Box, or in sweet-smelling Herbs, in Parterres. Rose-trees, intermixed with Pomegranates and Cornels, are very beautiful in a Hedge . . . what we are told Democritus very much condemned, namely, the inclosing a Garden with any Sort of Wall, I should not blame in the Case before us but am rather of Opinion, that it is very proper Defence against Malice or Rapine. Nor am I displeased with the placing ridiculous Statues in Gardens, provided they have nothing in them obscene.'

The Italian designer, as has been so clearly demonstrated by such writers as Edith Wharton, Inigo Triggs and Georgina Masson, covers his ground with man-made artifices of the kinds described

by Alberti. His plan follows throughout the dictates of geometry. Each part is related to the others, and, as can be seen in our illustration on page 7, to the house (in this case two separate pavilions). Indeed, G.A. Jellicoe wrote: 'It is as though more importance has been given to the idea of a garden than to the idea of a house.'

Great attention was paid to views. At the Villa Garzoni, at Collodi, high above the Arno, there is a two-fold theme: first, the view of the garden from below, and secondly, the view looking down the garden over to the countryside, illustrated above.

Both the aesthetics of fountains and the science of hydraulics were profoundly understood in Italy. Illustrated above are the massive eruptions from complex jets evolved by Orazio Olivieri in the mid-sixteenth century at the Villa d'Este—the *fontana dell' organo idraulico,* whose musical instrument was admired by both Evelyn and Montaigne—though the latter complained that it played but one tune.

As a contrast we show below the astonishing delicacy of the Fountain of the Lamps at the Villa Lante. Here, as was not unusual, the building of an aqueduct early in the sixteenth century by Signor Tomasi of Siena (so Montaigne tells us) enabled the fountains to play—a considerable and ingenious piece of engineering.

Today, when piped water is so common, we are inclined to forget that the fountain was utilitarian in its origins—a source of water; yet fountains were, from an early date, also designed as objects of beauty. In 1580 Montaigne wrote of the infinite abundance of fountains in Switzerland: 'There was no village or cross-road where there was not a beautiful one'. But the Italian Renaissance magnified the fountain into a work of art and fantasy:

> *Here a Chimaera opens wide his jaws*
> *And from her mouth a torrent throws . . .*
> *There with his arms, and watching as his game*
> *A brazen huntsman stands and takes his aim,*
> *To kill the prey, but shoots a harmless stream;*
> *A pleasing cheat, at which the wond'ring rout,*
> *At once with Laughter and applauses shout.*

At Villa Lante, too, is this massive sculpture of the fountain of the giants. Here the water is not thrown skyward, but tumbles, as in a waterfall, from between the claws of a crayfish—a rebus on the name of Cardinal Gambara (*gambero* means crayfish) who began the gardens in 1566.

Also at the Villa Lante is the contrasting Pegasus fountain (opposite) where the water springs in slender jets to fall back, arc-like, into a still pond.

If water can be projected into the sky to cause eternal surprise at such fine artifice, or be allowed to splash down like a controlled waterfall, it can also lie still and quiet, a mirror when the sun shines or a suggestion of unplumbable depth under leaden skies. The water garden at the Villa Gamberaia, shown opposite, displays this calmness.

The practice of covering a flat area with a geometrical pattern must surely be of great antiquity, and may well have in it the origins of ornamental gardening. Patterns traced out in elaborate paving, in different-coloured gravels and other minerals, and patterns marked out by edgings of box, rosemary and other dwarf shrubs, or, in those countries where it will grow, by short-mown grass, have been known as long as gardening itself. It is a theme with countless variations and one that continues to this day in spite of a couple of centuries of opposition from the 'natural' school of gardening.

It seems that the Italian Renaissance designers inherited the idea from the Romans, who might in their turn have had it from further east. It was developed somewhat later into the strapwork patterns of northern Europe (the Knot of Tudor gardens) and reached its greatest complexity and elegance in the *parterre* of eighteenth-century France. During the nineteenth century, elaboration was added by filling the spaces, or even marking out the patterns with highly coloured tender plants, raised in heat and bedded-out during summer.

One can only speculate how long this practice has been carried on in the Vatican gardens, shown below as they are today.

Perhaps the earliest form of scroll-work in gardening is dwarf box edging round flowerless compartments filled with coloured stones or gravel. Again we go to the Villa Lante for an example.

At the other extreme is the courtyard that has few plants and yet is essentially part of the garden. This example is in the Vatican gardens (opposite).

In the last illustration the courtyard was overlooked by a stone pine. This tree, with its spreading crown, contrasts throughout Mediterranean regions with the spire-like cypress, and thus introduces us to a contrast of tree forms which is a fundamental element in garden design. In different parts of the world, according to climate, different species of tree play their parts, and add distinctive qualities to the garden. In Persia, for example, the *chenar* or oriental plane is the spreading tree, while the cypress remains the narrow one. In much of northern Europe, where neither the cypress nor the stone pine is really hardy, such contrasts were not possible until the eighteenth century, when the narrow Lombardy poplar was introduced as a contrast to the oak—both being deciduous trees. The spreading Lebanon cedar, introduced to northern Europe in the seventeenth century, was without a narrow counterpart until the introduction of the western North American conifers in the early nineteenth century.

The stone pine has another curious connection with garden ornament. Its cone, the original pine apple, was a Roman fertility symbol, and from such a beginning found its way into Renaissance art as is seen in the finials at the Villa Garzoni, below. It is from these that the pine apple ornament so common in gardens today is descended; not from the tropical fruit originally named from a likeness to the cone.

'Nor am I displeased with the placing ridiculous statues in gardens, provided they have nothing in them obscene,' wrote Alberti. At Bomarzo, near Viterbo, in the middle of the sixteenth century the Duke Vicino Orsini implemented Alberti's precepts with such objects as this winged dragon fighting a lioness, a colossal tortoise, bears, a Roman soldier seized in the trunk of an elephant, giants and a fantastic head whose gaping features embody the mouth of hell.

The classical form of the Italian garden is always assumed to be comparatively flowerless, and so, to modern eyes, colourless. Miss Masson has, however, proved that this was not always so, and in the present century a number of gardeners have shown what a wide range of plants can be grown. The Villa Taranto on the shore of Lake Maggiore, shown opposite, has a garden of about a hundred acres planted by Captain McEacharn in the last few decades; the classical Italian garden is by no means disregarded, but is enriched with twentieth-century colour.

In the same garden the celebrated lotus pool, above, is in a formal setting surrounded by informality; the pergola (an ancient Italian device) is hung with wisteria, a nineteenth-century introduction from China.

By some, the garden of Isola Bella, rising out of Lake Maggiore and crowned with giant, sometimes statue-capped finials (opposite), is regarded as one of the greatest gardens of the world.

By others, on account of such ornate detail, as is displayed in the grotto opposite, it is considered 'a pyramid of sweetmeats ornamented with green festoons and flowers'.

The fact is that Isola Bella is a seventeenth-century garden, and
tends towards the baroque. In 1632, when work was begun by
Count Carlo Borromeo, there were no more than rocky islets; by
1671, when completed by his son after prodigious labours, the rocks

had become one of the sights of the 'grand tour'. Subsequent land-scape planting has to some extent obscured the original design. From the befinialled topmost level (which covers a giant water tank) the garden drops down in terraces to this *parterre* garden.

To understand the development of the formal garden in France it is necessary to go a little into its history. The spirit of the Renaissance had been brought north from Italy by Francis I in the early sixteenth century. The French had long been gardeners; it was the French monks who greatly improved English horticulture after the Norman conquest. However, the French garden was more frequently on level ground than were those in the hilly landscape of Italy. The French garden that was evolved by J. A. du Cerceaux (who died in 1585), Claude Mollet (whose *Théatre des Plans et Jardinages* was published posthumously in 1652) and his sons (one of whom, André, published *Le Jardin de Plaisir* in 1651) became something very different from its Italian origins. It was not so much an extension of the house as a separate entity surrounding the house, for which it was also a setting. It was, too, a setting for ceremonies and parades, for fêtes and masques. The style and the spirit of this type of garden is seen opposite in the engraving, dated 1629, by A. Bosse. Here are many of the Italian elements, yet with medieval remains such as the creeper-covered arbours.

In France the development of the garden was centred on the Court rather than, as in Italy, distributed among the popes, cardinals and nobility. In particular, Catherine de Medici after the death in 1559 of her husband, Henry II, the successor to Francis I, developed the Tuileries, acquired by Francis, and established a sort of central school of gardening which evolved a tradition of training not only in horticulture in its widest aspects, but in the architecture of garden design. In several families the tradition was passed on for three or even four generations. This continuity and gradual development was an important feature of the French formal garden. It was fortuitously strengthened by the birth, in 1613, probably in a house within the Tuileries, of André le Nôtre, whose father and grandfather were gardeners there; his godmother, too, was the wife of Claude Mollet. The young le Nôtre soon achieved a mastery of the arts of gardening excelling that of his contemporaries. In the French world of arts generally, he had a galaxy of contemporaries—Molière, Lully, Le Vau, Perrault, the Mansarts, Le Brun and, as expatriates, the Poussins and Claude.

Le Nôtre first demonstrated his skill in the grand manner for Nicolas Foucquet at Vaux-le-Vicomte. As a result, he became royal gardener, enjoying the favour of his master without break until his death in 1700. That master was Louis XIV, surely the

greatest royal patron of the arts of all times, who ruled from 1643–1710 (his reign therefore ranging over the English monarchs from Charles I to George I), and le Nôtre was thus able to develop a tradition to the third, perhaps fourth generation—an unusually long period.

The exquisite painting of 'The Lovers Crowned' by Fragonard, opposite, reflects the romantic sentimentality of Louis XIV period —a complete contrast to the rigidity of Bassin de Latone at Versailles.

The essential feature of the style of Le Nôtre was symmetry on either side of a great central vista. On the vast scale of his designs the cross vistas, set firmly at right angles, with their variation in detail, were also of considerable significance. Levels were rigidly controlled, and were normally few. This photograph of the Bassin de Latone at Versailles, with the view up the grand canal and beyond, displays these principles. Nearly always the vista is interrupted— in this case by the distant basin and statuary—but only temporarily, for one overlooks the break, and the eye follows the line until it disappears into the distant countryside. The design is an almost inhuman logical abstraction, quite unlike the Italian Renaissance garden.

Versailles has altered greatly, and it is well to look at it through contemporary eyes. This painting of the Piéce d'eaux des Suisse made in 1683 shows both the spacious scale on which Le Nôtre worked and his control of levels; here, as not infrequently, this is managed with great ramps. It also indicates the fine detail scrupulously carried out, another essential to his work.

A vista was usually framed between *bosquets*, or groves. These were formal woods, rectangular in shape. Within them was a geometrical arrangement of straight paths, often with a fountain or statue at their point of intersection. Here, at Versailles, is a pair of *bosquets*, framing the subsidiary (and terminated) vista of L'Allée des Marmousets.

The spaciousness and great impression of depth obtainable by flat sheets of water, planned architecturally and lined by trees, is seen at Sceaux (below); a 'vast conception that leaves one breathless'. Here there is no hint of intimacy either with man or with nature. It is an example of the human mind, at its most geometrical, demonstrating its mastery. As can be seen, this major work of Le Nôtre has fortunately been restored and replanted.

The horticultural embellishments of the period—the *parterres* and small pyramidal trees—have usually disappeared, so that today the ornamentation is primarily architectural. Thus, at Fontainbleau, in what the French call Le Jardin de Diane we see no garden in the present accepted sense—only a fountain and ornament.

The French were masters of hydraulics. Unlike the Italians, Le Nôtre was not usually able to take advantage of a steep fall in the site to give his fountains pressure. Yet fountains of the grandest kind, such as the famous Bassin d' Apollon at Versailles, below, were a feature of his gardens, as well as ingenious smaller devices.

Economic circumstances long ago caused the replacement of the elaborate *parterres* by lawns. But even the vegetable gardens were once laid out to a pattern that pleased the eye. The fruit trees were trained into alleyways or to form other interesting shapes, and, as in Italy, abstract patterns were woven in clipped box. All these features are to be seen in the remarkable reconstruction at Villandry (above).

Le Nôtre left neither plans nor notes on his work, which had greatly altered design since the publications of the Mollets. The French *savant* d'Argenville, however, published in 1709 *La Théorie et la Pratique du Jardinage*, which to some extent summarized the style of Le Nôtre. On the opposite page is reproduced the plate of a design for 'one of the noblest and most magnificent designs that can be' of about fifty or sixty acres in extent.

'The entrance of the great garden is by the descent of steps from the building [the house was raised so that the garden could be looked down upon], where you have a cross walk, terminated by grills of iron; and another double walk, which runs from one end of the garden to another, as do those two also by the walls which enclose the ground. Immediately under your eye are four pieces of *parterre*, with basons [with fountains] in their midst. These are accompanied by two open groves, adorned with bowling greens [these were not for playing the game, but were sunken lawns]. Beyond them is another large cross walk of yews, in the middle of which is the great bason. The head of this *parterre* is composed of four small grass plots, with edgings of box and yews, and above is a half-moon of palisades. This half-moon is parted into a goose-foot, and its alleys lead you to other basons and cabinets. Between each alley, it is set out with niches for figures. The groves are accompanied with two quincunces, set off with cabinets [arbours of wooden lattice work] and a hall in the middle, with figures. There is also a cross walk made by the palisades and trees of the groves, where are two basons, whose spouts are in a line with the great ones of the middle walk. Beyond are four groves, cut like St Andrew's cross. The two upon the right of the great walk contain a hall adorned with seats and figures, with a bowling-green, and another hall with branches of earth, which may serve for an amphitheatre, or theatre for playing comedies. In the two on the left there is an oval hall, with a bowling-green, different from the other, and a little hall of fountains, contrived in the four middles, without interrupting the line.

Beyond these groves is a large canal, reaching the whole breadth of the garden, in the midst of which is a group of figures, as Neptune with Tritons throwing one great spout, and many lesser every way. At each end of this canal the walls are opened, with cut ditches, to preserve the prospect. Further on are two large woods of high trees cut into a star, the alleys of which are double, and planted with trees that stand detached. In the middle of these woods are two different isles with figures and yews.

36

The general Disposition of a   Magnificent Garden all upon a level

At the end of the great walk, and beyond these woods, you meet with a low terrace wall, from whence you have a view of the country round about; a wet ditch runs the whole length of this wall; and in the front of the half-moon, at the end of the great walk, is made a cascade, which has three mask-heads and a sheet of water, that falls again into a water-work of two jets, the water of which comes from the canal, and supplies all the ditch without the garden.'

On either side of the house are the stables, granaries, menagerie, kitchen garden and so on, which we have not described.

The *parterre*, originally a Roman (or perhaps earlier) device for decorating a level space, was developed to an unexcelled degree of elaboration by the French, with whom it remains exceedingly popular, as may be seen in the illustration below—Vannes in 1960.

D'Argenville wrote that 'their compartments, and borders were taken from geometrical figures . . . They take various designs into their composition, as branched and flourished work, palms, foliage, hawk's-bills, sprigs, tendrils, volutes, knots [the earlier simpler strapwork-like designs], stalks, ties, chaplets, beads, husks, cartoozes, plumes . . .'

The French tradition of formality persists to this day. The arrangement of the flowers in the Roseraie de L'Hay would in the British Isles, for example, be considered old-fashioned and unnatural. In the background may be seen a type of structure, *treillage*, or arbour-work, in which the French formal gardener excelled. From thin lattice-work elaborate skeletal buildings were erected to form arbours, porticoes and summer-houses; they were 'often covered with rose-trees, jasmins, hony-suckles and wild vines for the conveniency of shade'.

Today it needs a great effort of imagination (or the second sight possessed by certain ladies) to separate from the camera-slung hordes of tourists something of the original eighteenth-century scene. Rigaud's engraving of 'Les Trois Fontaines', made about 1785, recalls the scene as it used to be.

The influence of Le Nôtre was widespread. The English Court in exile saw his work, and Charles II on his restoration emulated

it; it influenced the horticulturally minded Dutch; it is also reflected in such celebrated gardens as Schwetzingen in Germany, the Château de Boloeil in Belgium, in Russia at the Peterhof, in Sweden at the Palace of Drottningholm, and even in Spain at the Palace of La Granja. In all these places the gardens remain as a testimony to French genius; only in the British Isles has almost all trace of it been obliterated.

In Germany, Benrath, near Düsseldorf is a garden which has, on account of spacious avenues and fine trees combined with classical statuary, been compared to an old English formal garden. It surrounds a Rococo *schloss* built during the Seven Years War of 1756–63 (below).

The period that gave distinction to Austrian gardens was at the end of the seventeenth and the beginning of the eighteenth century, after J. B. Fischer von Erlach (who was followed by his son) returned from a long visit to Italy, where he absorbed the spirit of Italian baroque. The Upper Belvedere Palace is noted for its massive formal hedges and fine sculpture; the statuary of Lorenzo Matielli at the Schwarzenburg palace (opposite) is, too, of supreme quality.

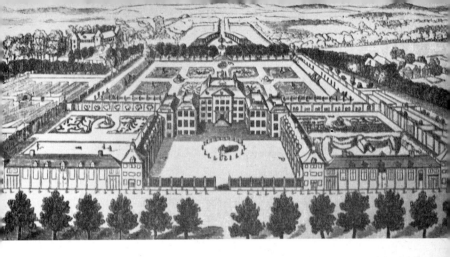

At Munich, the garden of the Nymphenburg (opposite) was originally in the French manner. At the end of the eighteenth century considerable additions in the English style were made, which included two extremely powerful fountains.

The Dutch style of gardening is not infrequently referred to, yet as far back as the seventeenth century travellers were commenting that it differed but little from the French, though it was remarked that Dutch gardens were 'more confined, more covered with frivolous ornaments, and more intersected with still and often muddy pieces of water'. This contemporary engraving of the garden of the palace of Loo (it was made by William II and Mary) shows the French influence. It is significant too that extensive 'Dutch' garden-making in England (including the alteration at Hampton Court) was carried out by George London, who had studied garden design in France. As late as 1764 Humphry Repton as a young man described the Dutch gardens seen from the canals as almost flowerless, with beds arranged in patterns edged with dwarf box and filled with red brick-dust, charcoal, yellow sand, green broken glass and spars. The Dutch influence was not really in design, but in horticulture. The Dutch were among the first introducers of foreign plants—especially bulbs. It was to study in their botanical gardens that George London visited Holland, and it was with rare plants from William Bentinck's Soesdyke that Hampton Court was enriched. The Dutch were, and still are, masters of cultivation.

45

The essential qualities of the Dutch garden, those of intimacy, ornamentation and floriculture, are shown in many Dutch paintings. This town garden, probably in Amsterdam, was painted by Cornelis Troost (1697–1750).

Italy, France and Holland all have Rome as a source of culture: these countries have a classical common denominator. When we move to the Iberian peninsula we find new elements, coming from north Africa and beyond. The detail (opposite) from Casa del Pilatos at Seville indicates this Moorish spirit, now so foreign to the more northerly tradition.

Portugal faces the Atlantic breezes, which have many effects on its gardens and botany. Vegetation is much more lush than in Spain, and in many places such plants as camellias flourish. Moorish occupation has left its mark, but so have commerce and Portugal's one-time overseas empire. The feature of Portugal, so often commented on, is the bright colouring both of its buildings and of its gardens. Illustrated below is the pink mid-eighteenth-century Queluz. The garden is laid out in the French style with ornate clipped *parterres* and statuary which has yet been assimilated in the Portuguese manner.

Opposite is the Quinta de Fronteira—held to be a fine example of the essentially gay Portuguese garden. The ornate clipped *parterre*, palm-shaded, lies below buildings with ornate facings.

The terrace walk (opposite) is an example of Portuguese elaboration: coloured and painted tiles (*azulejos*), statuary and medallions are decorated with pelargoniums.

Against this richly ornamented wall stands a fountain, shown below, which plays into what might be described as a *parterre* worked in stone upon water.

It is in Spain that the full Oriental style shows itself in Europe. The Alhambra (opposite), 'this Moorish fortress-palace left on southern Spanish soil, like some beautiful and curious shell stranded by a far-receding tide', was begun high above Seville in 1248. Typical are the water-centred courtyards, whose simple design contrasts with the architectural extravagance of Italy, though walls and roofs are brilliantly coloured.

The structural simplicity of the Alhambra is well seen in the fountain below.

The same simplicity of form (not of surfaces or decoration) is seen in the courtyard of the Generaliffe, another thirteenth-century building near the Alhambra. Here is a quiet shady place, whose gently splashing fountains are very different from the foaming, soaring or elaborate jets of Italy. The bowl in the foreground is the lotus fountain, another symbol that we are, though within Europe geographically, outside it spiritually.

Though really outside our terms of reference, it is interesting to look at an eastern example of this kind of garden. The Indian seventeenth-century garden tomb of Mumtaz Mahal was originally planned as a tribute to India's womanhood, which accounts for its feminine quality.

Paradoxically, it is in India that we find the most remarkable formal garden of the early twentieth century—that designed at New Delhi for the Viceroy of India by Sir Edwin Lutyens, and now used as the President's Residence. As Robert Byron wrote, like the elaborate and formal water-systems of the Moguls and Italians, it is strictly architectural. Indeed, in many ways the disparate elements of both racial traditions are united by the powerful genius of Lutyens in a

new conception of formality. This work inevitably leads us back to the British Isles, for, in a period when the natural garden apparently reigned supreme, such men as Lutyens and Peto made the only original English contributions to the design of formal gardens; the sixteenth and seventeenth-century work, fine as it was, had been based on Le Nôtre, and the nineteenth-century efforts had been mostly imitative.

If in the twentieth century the architectural garden reached its
ultimate in Sir Edwin Lutyens's Indian design, the country of his
birth had not only abandoned but wantonly destroyed most of its
formal gardens during the latter part of the eighteenth century.
There are remains here and there. The general lay-out is still intact
at Melbourne in Derbyshire. Studley Royal and Bramham Park in
Yorkshire show us something of the manner. But one of the most

interesting is Powis Castle (illustrated on these pages). Here is a garden falling steeply in terraces, in the Italian manner, laid out by a Dutchman from the court of William III. Early eighteenth-century additions, and more recent planting also take advantage of the fine horticultural situation. What were probably neatly clipped pyramids and cones in the Dutch style have today grown into massive specimens, which, though presumably bearing no relation to the original designer's intentions, now lend great majesty to the garden. Shown opposite are the Italian-like fall of be-statued terraces, looking not over the Roman *campagna* but over the Severn Vale.

Chatsworth is a palimpsest of tastes in garden design. Fortunately, the great cascade in the style of Le Nôtre, by his pupil Grillet, still remains. The temple at its head (above) from which the waters now stream torrentially in every direction, was added in 1703, and was probably designed by William Archer.

The clipping of trees and shrubs—topiary work, from the Roman *topiarius*, who as head gardener was then responsible for the work—is an essential part of the formal garden. At Levens Hall, Westmorland, the topiary garden was begun by a certain Beaumont in about 1689, though, of course, altered and replanted subsequently. This type of work is generally considered to be Dutch.

As a contrast to the whimsicality of Levens, the simplicity of the modern topiary garden at Hidcote Manor, Gloucestershire, is satisfying. One aspect of it is illustrated here.

The Dutch style is also recalled by the formal sunk pond garden at the side of Kensington Palace. This, with the beautifully trained pleached lime arbour which partially surrounds it, accords well with the palace buildings, and was made in 1908.

The Dutch use of ornamental containers, in which were grown exotic plants, goes back at least to the early seventeenth century. It is resorted to with satisfactory effect around a rectangular pool in the modern garden at Talbot Manor, Norfolk.

During the nineteenth century a number of old gardens which had been landscaped were in part restored to a formal design. W. A. Nesfield was frequently engaged on this work, and this garden at Easton Neston, Northamptonshire, was restored by him.

Wrest Park, Bedfordshire, was a great formal garden begun in the late seventeenth century. Some of the buildings and waterworks remain. The beautiful *parterre* in the formal manner, aptly surrounding old statuary, is modern. It is here viewed, as was intended with *parterres*, from above.

Also looked down upon is the effective circular *parterre* in the French manner in a Surrey garden. Here it is most satisfactorily combined with a herbaceous border.

In the United States of America there were two original sources of garden design. The earlier, the south-western, was Spanish, but elsewhere it was principally English, or European. Oak Hill Garden, Loudoun County, Virginia (above), with its simple formality, is ideally suited to the calm classicism of the house.

An equally appropriate setting to a more modest house is the box-edged flower-filled *parterre* at Gunston Hall, near Alexandria, Virginia (opposite), with its undemonstrative charm.

A more original classicism is seen on the long seat standing in front of white-stemmed trees in the garden of the late Homer St Gaudens—a style redolent of the early twentieth century.

Old Westbury Gardens on Long Island, belonging to the early years of this century, are avowedly designed in the manner of the English eighteenth century. How effectively this has been done can be seen from this detail.

As a contrast to the calm of the four American gardens just mentioned, Longwood, Pennsylvania, recalls Renaissance brilliance and

virtuosity executed with twentieth-century vigour. These elements are displayed in the huge conservatory and the fountain garden.

We have suggested that the design of British formal gardens was at its best in the first part of the present century. Harold Peto was a masterly exponent of the style. In his own garden at Iford Manor, Wiltshire (above), the colonnaded terrace which he designed to include his statuary and other works of art, complies with his belief that stone and plants should be combined in the right proportions. Peto merged his formality into the surroundings with great skill.

Peto's best-known work is probably the long canal, or perhaps more accurately, cascade, that leads, as a stepped avenue of water between trees, from the house to the lake at Buscot Park, Berkshire (below). Simple in conception, it is, like all his work, beautifully executed in detail.

Of about the same period, and a typically Scandinavian adaptation of the classical style, was the garden of Carl Milles, the Swedish sculptor, on the island of Lidingon, near Stockholm (above). It ingeniously retains the old and very irregular pines and birches.

One of the most remarkably lavish English gardens was that made for Sir Philip Sassoon at Port Lympne during the nineteen-twenties. This view of the bathing pool shows its remarkable situation overlooking the Kent Marshes.

We introduced Lutyens's work with an example showing it at its most complex and extended (pp. 56–57). At Ashby St Ledgers, Northamptonshire, is one of the most interesting of his gardens designed around a group of domestic buildings. Here, outstandingly simple, is the canal that links it with the surrounding landscape.

The inspiration of nature

The more one examines the origins of the English landscape garden the more obscure they become. Indeed, the revolution in gardening seems to presage rather than follow the change in the philosophers' views upon nature. These were first publicly expressed in such works as Shaftesbury's *Characteristics* (1711–14), Kames's *Elements of Criticism* (1762) and Burke's *Philosophical Enquiry into . . . the Sublime and Beautiful* (1756–7). Yet Joseph Addison in *Remarks on Several Parts of Italy in the Years 1701, 1702, 1703* concludes that the only merit of the Italian gardens is that they indicate the origins of the style of Le Nôtre. In the same work he wrote of Vesuvius: 'There is nothing about Naples, nor indeed any part of Italy, which deserves our attention so much as this mountain.' In 1667 Dryden had written: 'High objects, it is true, attract the sight; but it looks up with pain on craggy rocks and barren mountains!'

'I must confess I was most pleased with a beautiful prospect that none of them [the itineraries] have mentioned, which lies at about a mile distance from the town. It opens on one side into the Roman Campania, where the eye loses itself on a smooth spacious plain. On the other side is a more broken and interrupted scene, made up of an infinite variety of inequalities and shadowings, that naturally arise from an agreeable mixture of hills, groves, and valleys. But the most enlivening part of all, is the river Teverone, which you see at about a quarter of a mile's distance, throwing itself down a precipice . . .' So Addison continued.

This was the type of scene loved by the French expatriate painters which was to permeate the whole spirit of the landscape garden, the spirit which was much later incongruously described by W. Hutchinson in his *Excursion to the Lakes* of 1776: 'The paintings of *Pousin* describe the nobleness of Uls-water; the works of *Salvator Rosa* express the romantic and rocky scene of Keswick, and the tender elegant touch of *Claude Lorraine*, and *Smith*, pencil forth the rich variety of Windermere.'

These names, Poussin, Salvator and Claude (if not Smith) echo and re-echo throughout the discussions on the landscape garden throughout the eighteenth century. So does, in the earlier part of the century, the word 'irregularity'. In 1685 Sir William Temple has written: 'What I have said of the best forms of gardening, is meant only of such as are in some sort regular; for there may be other forms wholly irregular that may, for aught I know, have more beauty than any of the others.' He goes on to describe what he has heard of Chinese gardens and the quality the Chinese termed *sharawadgi*.

Sharawadgi is a word that was often used in the following century. But, except for the at first anarchical introduction of irregularity, which was quite, as we now know, unrelated to the principles of Chinese garden design, and the charming conceits of *chinoiserie*—also a largely imagined version of Chinese art and architecture—it is important to realize that China played no part in the origins of the English landscape garden.

Obscure though the sparks that set off the movement are, we have seen how an entirely new conception of gardening was coming into existence. Horticulture and (except incidentally) architecture played no part in it; most of its early practitioners were concerned with poetry, philosophy, aesthetics, painting, and historical or literary allusions. Their aim was to create illusions of ideal worlds, which they professed to think was inspired by irregular nature herself. Here, indeed, was an entirely new form of gardening: it was landscape painting in which the earth itself was moved to form ideal contours, water was controlled to form perfect lakes or romantic waterfalls, and trees were planted to grow into nature's forests.

From these early conceptions have developed the numerous varieties of landscape, or irregular, gardens, that at the present time dominate garden design. At first the movement spread to France as *le jardin anglais* or even *le jardin anglais-chinois*; Horace Walpole was pretty curt about the manner in which the French carried it out. When J. C. Loudon visited Italy in 1820, gardens were pointed out to him as *veramente Inglese*, with which he, too, disagreed.

Two distinct principles of design can be traced throughout the history of the landscape garden. The first is the purely idyllic version: the reshaping of natural resources, and the exploitation of native trees and shrubs to form an echo of a Virgilian or Spenserian pastoral scene, or of the Roman *campagna*. Such was the ideal of Kent or Shenstone. Good roadside landscaping today evolves from this.

The second was something more imaginative; it might be called (to use a modern term) the plantsman's version. The microcosm was created with much more elaborate and exotic materials. Probably the progenitor of this mode was Hamilton's Pains Hill, where his landscape was filled with rare trees of all kinds, and where, probably, azaleas (freshly introduced from North America) were

80

first used on an extensive scale. This style leads us to Sheffield Park in England or the Magnolia Gardens in the United States.

The first practical gardeners to have introduced irregularity seem to have been Charles Bridgeman, who became Royal Gardener, and who died in 1738, and Stephen Switzer (1682?–1745), who was trained in the school of London and Wise (he worked, for instance, on the original formal garden of Vanbrugh's Blenheim Palace to the masterly design of Henry Wise). Switzer's views were summed up in his *Ichnographia Rustica* (1718). In it he describes how George London, when at Vanbrugh's Castle Howard, had prescribed within Wray wood: 'a star which would have spoil'd the wood, but that his Lordship's [the third Earl of Carlisle] superlative genius prevented it and to the great advancement of the design has given it that labyrinth diverting model we now see it; and it is at this time a proverb at that place, York against London, in allusion to the design of a Londoner and Mr London the designer'. This event took place some time after 1699 when Vanbrugh arrived on the scene at Castle Howard, and it is not impossible that it was he, romantically inclined, who made the suggestion to his Lordship.

Switzer also uses such phrases as 'that inexpressible somewhat to be found in the Beauty of Nature'. We can, therefore, for convenience take his work as the beginning of the landscape movement. But how rudimentary it was we can see from his own design (below) for 'the manor of Paston divided and planted into rural Gardens'.

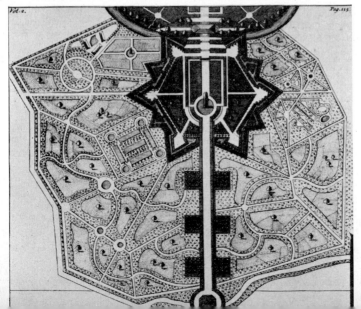

The key to the development of the landscape garden was the introduction of the ha-ha. By its use, the surrounding landscape could be apparently merged into the more ornamental grounds adjoining the mansion by means of an invisible barrier to stock and deer—whose browsing within sight of the windows now added rural delights to the scene. It was no more than a dry ditch, one side of which was vertical (drawing above), and appears to have been an

invention of some antiquity; possibly to trap deer who could jump down the sharp drop but then could not get up again. Or again, possibly, it was used in fortifications. Certainly the French employed it in their formal gardens, and provided the name: 'a large and deep ditch . . . lined on both sides to sustain the earth, and prevent the getting over, which surprises the eye upon coming near it, and makes one cry Ah! Ah! from whence it takes its name'.

Who introduced the ha-ha as a device to fence in the formal garden is not known with precision. The credit is usually given to the royal gardener Charles Bridgeman. During the eighteenth and early nineteenth centuries many hundreds of miles of it were constructed. Typically, it could be built in the manner seen at Lacock Abbey, in Wiltshire (below left). Sometimes (as at Blenheim Palace) the design was altogether more massive, and intended, one feels, to guard against some giant auroch rather than the domestic cow. Elsewhere, the wall might only be of light brickwork.

The ha-ha is an instrument of art rather than a work of art in itself, for its essence is to be unseen. The only point at which a decorative feature that can embellish it is where it is bridged by a roadway. An example of this, elaborated into a feature, is seen at Ham House at Richmond (below).

Rousham in Oxfordshire was designed by William Kent for General Dormer in the early seventeen-twenties. The general plan remains today very much as it originally was, and contrasts violently with the formal gardens still being constructed—though, even in these, simple lawns were tending to replace elaborate *parterres*.

The site is on the steepish bank of the River Cherwell, which makes two sharp bends. Except for three main vistas, the winding paths and plantings accord with, and are not imposed upon, the shape and lie of the land. The most striking building is the Praeneste Arcade (above). The view of this down a glade, to which it is

obliquely set, from a giant statue of Apollo, breaks entirely new ground in garden design. There are architectural objects set around, such as a pyramid and the temple known as Townsende's building. Even the old bridge over the river is brought into the scene. It is quite wrong to regard these buildings as follies. They are mostly commemorative or symbolic—as they were in other similar gardens of the period. Their significance is often lost today, when we have little knowledge of the classics. There can be no mistake, however, over the memorial to Ringwood (above), 'an otter hound of extraordinary sagacity'.

The garden of Stourhead, begun around a series of ponds in a bleak, treeless Wiltshire landscape by Henry Hoare in the seventeen-forties, also remains as he intended it to be, but is probably improved by subsequent plantings. The whole design centres around the lake (opposite). It was well described by a versifier:

> *Throughout the various scenes above, below,*
> *Lawns, walks, and slopes, with verdant carpets glow:*
> *On the clear mirror float the inverted shades*
> *Of woods, plantations, wildernesses, glades*
> *Rocks, bridges, temples, grottos and cascades.*

Stourhead is of the sophisticated style of landscape garden. Whereas at Rousham the trees and shrubs are mostly natives, the Hoare family has traditionally, through succeeding generations, planted exotics, so that the scene is often brilliantly coloured. The statuary is exceptionally fine: an example is John Cheere's River God (above), lamp-lit in a dark grotto.

The buildings at Stourhead are distinguished, and some are on a considerable scale. It is the Pantheon, designed by Henry Flitcroft, and of notable workmanship, that dominates the pictures on page

87. The temple of Flora, with its beautiful Doric portico, is more secluded; it contains an urn honouring Flora and her attendants. In front of it is the Paradise Well.

The English landscape garden in due course became the vogue in France. British—usually Scottish—gardeners were much in demand in the decades before the Revolution. A writer of the time claimed that French gardens were being replanted *à l'Anglaise* 'with a warmth more common to the mania of imitation than the genius of invention'.

The very English inventors of the *ferme ornée* could never have imagined that the French *anglomanie* would produce anything so extravagant as the hamlet in the Trianon (above) where Marie Antoinette posed as *la belle fermière*.

It was generally agreed by English travellers that Ermenonville was the finest French garden in the English manner. Arthur Young, that connoisseur of the English garden, praised the management of the lakes, which contained the Island of Poplars (below), on which stood Rousseau's tomb. This garden was laid out by the Vicomte Girardin in the seventeen-seventies.

The most prolific designer of British landscape gardens from the seventeen-fifties until his death in 1783 was Lancelot Brown. His aim seems to have been to achieve an air of placidity. Rarely did he attempt a dramatic landscape; one feels that at heart he would have regarded a Stourhead as in rather bad taste. He was a master of the calm lake, usually without apparent end or beginning, often contrived out of some insignificant stream. A typical and eternally peaceful example is Compton Verney (below) in the heart of Warwickshire.

It must always be held against Brown and, to a lesser extent, his successor Humphry Repton, that they were considerable vandals and destroyed many of the old formal gardens—the great *parterre* at Blenheim is an example—and avenues beyond count.

Their work was eventually attacked for dullness; it is now often absorbed almost unaltered into the typical (and delightful) rural English landscape. Corsham Court, Wiltshire (above), on which both worked, shows both its imaginative weakness and its pleasing dignity.

By the middle of the nineteenth century gardeners in the warmer southern and western coastal districts had realized that plants formerly considered tender could be grown out of doors. The result was that trees and shrubs from the Himalayas (notably those collected in 1847–51 by J. D. Hooker), China, South America and even the Australian continent, were planted informally, sometimes to elaborate the landscape of a Brown or Repton: indeed, the latter foresaw the much greater use that could be made of exotic plants.

This accession of new plants coincided with, or perhaps itself changed, the whole spirit of landscape gardening. The allusions to mythology and history in scenes and buildings were replaced by an interest in the trees, shrubs and plants themselves. The pride of an owner was no longer in some chaste temple, but in an exotic Tibetan rhododendron.

This delight in exotics is displayed in the singularly un-English appearance of Abbotsbury (opposite), close to the sea in Dorset, and begun in the late eighteenth century, where such plants as camellias and 'palms' have now reached great size.

One of the most effective examples of the use of trees, shrubs and other naturalized plants to achieve both the permanent design and seasonal colour is at Sheffield Park, Sussex (below). Here they entirely transform with their rich and subtle elaboration an earlier landscape in which both Brown and Repton had taken a hand.

Leonardslee (below) in Sussex is a twentieth-century garden formed in a valley around a stream and a series of ponds. This was one of the gardens in which the plutocracy of the early twentieth century bred rhododendrons in a manner formerly reserved for race-horses. Here, as in all landscape gardening, great imagination was needed, for the garden was designed to reach perfection in the distant future. The formal garden, on the other hand, made its full effect within a year or two, as plants were secondary to stone and water.

The landscape garden could be on an immense scale. At Bodnant (opposite), in North Wales, the design is both intricate and yet so vast that it retains significance undwarfed by the mountains of Snowdonia.

Not far from Bodnant, where the wide River Conway winds below the garden, is—or rather was—at Bulkeley Mill (above), a garden made by the late A. T. Johnson on a scale matching the small stream on whose banks it stands. Yet it is in no way a miniature of the great garden; it is an application of the same principles refined, to make a garden both of the utmost interest to a plantsman and of considerable charm of design within an acre or two. Johnson's example, owing to his writings, was of considerable influence on the development of the small informal garden.

These natural gardens do not, of course, always consist of trees, shrubs and naturalized bulbs. It is possible, with comparatively little labour, to use certain herbaceous plants. Particularly successful arc some of the Asiatic primulas. One or two species that grow on streamsides will maintain themselves for many years virtually unattended. An example of their vigorous growth is seen at Trengwainton (below) in Cornwall.

Though most of the earliest gardens in which exotic plants were naturalized were in the milder districts, where there is heavy rainfall, one of the most influential was that made by G. F. Wilson on the cold, dry and thin soil of Surrey at Wisley (below), which has become the Royal Horticultural Society's garden. Here, among native heath and woodland of birch and oak, is an example that has been followed in the gardens of many well-to-do London commuters who, during the last few decades, have built their houses in similar countryside.

A remarkable garden is that of Mount Usher (above) in Ireland. Begun nearly a century ago, and laid out on either side of a river, it is notable for the remarkably rich variety of plants that it contains. Scarcely, perhaps, a landscape garden, it yet ranks as an informal garden of real artistic consequence.

Among the informal gardens, we should include arboreta and pineta, which are primarily collections of exotic trees but are usually so laid out that they are considerable achievements as works of garden art. One of the earliest is Dropmore in Buckinghamshire, begun in 1795. The placing of the huge and dominating South

American araucaria or monkey-puzzle tree (above) is visually most exciting.

The North American landscape garden was pioneered by Andrew Downing, under the influence of J. C. Loudon, who in turn based his theories on those of 'Capability' Brown as developed by Humphry Repton. The native material in the cooler regions is fundamentally the same as in much of Europe, though infinitely richer. The exotic, particularly Asiatic, is the same, though its use is more localized by climate. Where the American landscape garden attains a singular quality of its own is in South Carolina, with its native water cypresses, giant evergreen magnolias, dogwoods and live oaks draped with Spanish moss. In the Magnolia Gardens (opposite) and Middleton Gardens (pages 104–105)—both old gardens— these are combined with the more usual plantings of rhododendrons, azaleas, Asiatic magnolias, wisterias and camellias to form a luxurious vegetation singularly distinct from the restraint of a Brown landscape.

The inspiration of symbolism

Gardening, it is said, was introduced to Japan in the seventh century from China, where horticulture and floriculture are of great antiquity. China, particularly in its inaccessible central and western parts, was—and still is—a richly stocked store-house upon which gardeners have drawn from early times to select and improve plants. Many of the plants at first thought to be natives of Japan or even Persia have since been traced back to western China. The same can be said of such fruits as the peach and black mulberry.

Chinese gardens have given us, in addition to plants, painting and poetry, that architectural illusion known as *chinoiserie*.

The Japanese, however, developed their garden art and plants in comparative isolation for century after century. Kaempfer first described the Japanese gardens in the late seventeenth century, but it was not until the mid-nineteenth century that their subtleties became known to the western world.

The Japanese garden is fundamentally based on nature and natural forms, but interpreted in a manner totally distinct from the western conception of these terms. The garden is in no way imitative of natural scenery, but is an entity on its own, symbolic of nature and its elemental forces and qualities. At the same time it attempts to be a work of art having permanence in its own right, contrived with an artifice that has been evolved over the centuries. It is achieved by apparent simplicity; perhaps no more than rocks set in sand. It may be intimately connected with philosophy in its design, and contemplation in its daily usage. It is frequently, as in Renaissance Italy, almost an integral part of the house.

This intimacy is seen in the late-sixteenth-century garden at Kyoto (opposite), where the typical and best-known constituents of a Japanese garden—water, stone, trees, stone lantern and a bridge—are present. 'Dry' landscapes and rock gardens are, however, also constructed.

The drinking of tea was inevitably connected with gardens; the same close association between tea-house and garden is seen in the picture at Omuro, Kyoto (above).

Here most of the same elements are present in the garden of an inn (opposite), the principal being water, the whole furnished preponderantly with vegetation.

As a contrast to the last figure, this view in the garden of the Katsura Imperial Villa shows a landscape of infinite variation composed of water and stones.

Water, bridge, stone and lantern against trees give a vista of infinite variation in a garden at Katsura.

There is a striking superficial likeness between a modern Japanese garden at Kyoto (below) and the type of natural bog garden advocated by Reginald Farrer. As one of his first visits was to Japan (of which he wrote with great enthusiasm), one feels that he was greatly influenced by the Japanese tradition.

Bridges are of great significance. In our previous illustrations examples have been of moderate size, but in the garden of Kameido Shrine, Tokyo (below), they are of much greater consequence. Here, too, are pergola-like structures draped with creepers, overhanging the water.

Very great attention is paid to the design of fences (one authority gives a list of some thirty imaginatively named kinds) and gates. Examples of both in a garden at Hamamatsu are seen opposite.

Chinese influence on western garden design has not been significant. The eighteenth-century cult of '*chinoiserie*' was not based on any real understanding of Chinese architecture; nor, at that period, were more than a few of the plants essential to Chinese gardens grown outside China. Since the early nineteenth century western gardens have, on the other hand, become greatly indebted to the wealth both of species and florists' forms of Chinese plants that have been introduced.

From the late nineteenth century onwards, however, a modest number of genuinely Japanese gardens, usually built by Japanese designers, have been made in the West. An example in Hertfordshire is illustrated below. Furthermore, the influence of Japanese art on the French impressionist painters of the late nineteenth century was great. It is seen, for example, in the garden pictures of Monet, which in turn influenced garden designers such as Miss Gertrude Jekyll.

The Japanese mastery of simplicity in design, uniting elemental water, natural plant (lotus) and rock forms, and wrought stone, is seen in the detail opposite of the Priest's garden, Kyoto.

The inspiration of flowers

It is difficult to know for how long the enjoyment of plants for the beauty of their flowers or foliage has existed. Their practical uses, as herbal medicine, as fragrance to combat the smells of unhygienic civilizations, or as material for expendable garlands, are more frequently referred to by old writers. Perhaps the Chinese, the Persians and the Mexicans were aware of their innate qualities before, in Renaissance times, they were clearly appreciated in Europe.

Even then, it cannot be said that flowers initially inspired the art of garden making. In the grand gardens they usually had to compete with coloured minerals.

Flowers were probably grown for their own sakes in less sophisticated gardens, gardens in the inconsequential country world to which Herrick was banished:

> *I sing of brooks, of blossoms, birds, and bowers:*
> *Of April, May, of June, and July-flowers . . .*

By the late seventeenth century the cultivation of exotics by 'curious' (that is, inquiring) gardeners had become the rage, and it continued discreetly within walled gardens during the landscape era, when flowers were banished from sight. Then, by the mid-nineteenth century, the fashion of bedding-out had brought flowers back, but flowers of an impermanent nature.

The present-day importance of flowers (and their form and foliage) as an integral part of garden design can be traced back to the prolific writings of William Robinson (1838–1935) and Gertrude Jekyll (1843–1935), though there was nothing particularly novel in their ideas. They urged greater use of herbaceous perennials to replace the annually bedded-out and half-hardy plants. Miss Jekyll was an artist, and was one of the first to see very clearly the aesthetic value and possibilities both of the colours and of the architectural forms of plants.

Both William Robinson and Gertrude Jekyll learned much from the unsophisticated yet traditional cottage garden, whose delights came from flowers and probably one or two shrubs or small trees. Such is the garden at Bickleigh, Devon (below).

Robinson particularly urged the use of climbing plants on walls. On the beautifully coloured, but architecturally undistinguished, walls of Sissinghurst Castle in Kent the late Miss Sackville-West made most enjoyable plantings of roses (opposite).

Today, it surprises us that the potentialities of the narcissus as a plant for development and extensive naturalizing were not appreciated until the late part of the nineteenth century. They are used to their full advantage in the Wilderness Garden at Hampton Court, illustrated on the next two pages.

During the present century the form and leafage of plants has become increasingly appreciated. There is, for example, the extremely interesting foliage of *Rodgersia pinnata* (above), a plant whose flower is insignificant.

The hardy cyclamen throws up its pink flowers in late summer, then come the leaves, their sombre green relieved by silver markings, and through them arise snowdrops in the New Year: above them, perhaps, a spring-flowering tree may provide the needed shade.

Miss Jekyll campaigned for the mixed flower border carefully planned to show a sequence of colour schemes. Her ideals spread far and wide, and are beautifully carried out at Old Westbury (above) on Long Island.

When the climate is more or less frost-free, the range of plants formed with fierce geometry is greatly increased by species from South America, the Australian continent and South Africa, which can be grown out of doors, as they are here at Tresco in the Isles of Scilly.

As a complete contrast in form and colour to the 'geometrical' exotics is the European willow gentian (*Gentiana asclepiadea*)—opposite. Everything about it is gentle and graceful.

Flowers can be made to perform tricks, though the desirability or otherwise of this divides gardeners into two parties. We feel, however, we should be fair to both sides and so show below a rose trained into a bow (or a shamrock?) from the Roseraie de l'Hay.

The richness of flower and foliage, colour and plant form, is splendidly displayed at Sissinghurst Castle in Kent (opposite).

Flowers have been the essential of window-box gardening since, and no doubt before, Martial referred to the art in Rome some 1,900 years ago. How cleverly they may be combined with balustrading is seen in the photograph below, which shows a house front in the West End of London.

The architectural quality of ferns was more widely appreciated in the nineteenth century than today, when the fernery has almost become extinct. This fine example of tree-ferns and *Woodwardia* at Tatton Park, Cheshire, serves also to make our apology for not including (because of lack of space) examples of the inspiration of glass, which should range from Wren orangeries to Paxtonian conservatories.

The need for shelter

In Pliny's garden there was an alcove with a couch on which he rested. From under this couch sprang fountains, the water spurting as if pressed out by the weight of the reclining figure; he had, too, a marble summer house opening on to a green enclosure. The idea of sheltered and enclosed resting places must be of great antiquity, and the buildings to provide them have been carried out in every conceivable form. With them we may include sheltered walks such as creeper-covered arbours, pergolas, yew walks and pleached alleyways. The purpose of these was, in the country of their origin, to provide shade from the sun's heat. The name 'shade houses' was used for them in Jacobean England, where their purpose was more frequently protection from easterly winds or showers.

The more substantial of these buildings in the eighteenth-century formal gardens had become known as belvederes: 'the ends and extremities of a park are beautified with pavilions of masonry, which the French call belvederes, or pavilions of Aurora, which are as pleasant to rest one's selves in, after a long walk, as they are to the eye, for the handsome prospect that they yield; they serve also to retire into for shelter when it rains. The word *Belvedere* is Italian, and signifies a beauteous prospect, which is properly given to these pavilions; for that always being upon some eminence, they open and command the country round about.'

Banqueting houses were an introduction to northern Europe from Renaissance Italy, and were used not for banqueting as we now understand the term, but for 'entertainments and light refreshments' within the precincts of the garden.

The gazebo—or rather its name—is a peculiar English invention of the eighteenth century. Like the belvederes, of which it might be described as a miniature form, it is a small building from which one may survey the countryside (or discreetly observe the comings and goings along a road). Not infrequently in walled gardens it was an upstairs apartment that rose above the walls. Possibly the name is a shortening of 'gaze-about', or it may be a mock Latin word.

The imitation temple, derived from the genuine temples of Greece and Rome, was a frequent ornament or 'eye-catcher', particularly in the eighteenth-century landscape garden. These buildings often engaged the serious attention of distinguished architects.

The original shade-giving structures were 'herbers' or arbours—greenery trained over a framework, either to form a small shelter in the corner of a garden, or quite frequently taking the form of shady corridors. These are far from common today, the pergola in particular having now taken the form of a widely spread series of arches constructed for the purpose of displaying a variety of roses, clematis, and other climbing plants.

In later times such walks were made from lime trees that were 'pleached', that is, with the young shoots trimmed and intertwined (plaited), and trained over an iron framework of arches. Sometimes the trunks of the trees themselves form the erect frame, and the annual shoots form the covering. This can be seen at St Fagan's Castle, Cardiff and, as the picture below shows, in winter the sun shines through and warms the walk, while in summer the leaves give shade from the sun.

Even more substantial shelters formed from living material were arbours of clipped evergreens. There is such a 'building' in the centre of the yew garden at Rous Lench in Worcestershire, shown above. This may well go back to the seventeenth century, though much of the rest of the topiary is more recent.

The great era of small garden buildings began in the late seventeenth century. Le Nôtre had his belvederes and Inigo Jones designed his rare pavilions as flawless pieces of architecture. In England Sir John Vanbrugh produced masterpieces at Stowe and, in 1724, the extremely fine Temple of the Four Winds (shown above), at Castle Howard in Yorkshire.

Substantial garden buildings, too, were constructed in France. Illustrated below is the 'Folie d'Artois' at Bagatelle in the Bois de Boulogne. It stands, not in a formal garden in the style of Le Nôtre, but in an early *jardin anglais* designed by the Scotsman William Blaikie.

We have already referred to the word 'gazebo' as an eighteenth-century invention, and indeed, these buildings were greatly in vogue during that period. Two-storeyed buildings which qualified for that title (and for the modern 'observation post'!) were, however, built long before. The following pages illustrate one of the two that stand on what was formerly the entrance court of Montacute House in Somerset. They were built in the late sixteenth century when Renaissance emotions were stirring English craftsmen. Observers from within buildings of such grace, gazing on the gardens, the park and the comings and goings of a house, could surely not be called Peeping Toms!

As the formal garden declined and the landscape became fashionable, buildings of every kind were scattered about as eye-catchers. Few late-eighteenth-century gardens were without them, designed by architects of the quality of the Adams and downwards. Mock ruined castles were erected, as at Hagley, but these scarcely qualify as places within which one might sit. A charming classical temple, of the late eighteenth century, is shown below. It was added to the old garden at Blickling, Norfolk.

This distinguished American example of a 'temple in miniature' which is used as a shade house, is in the garden of Sweet Briar College, Virginia.

Eclecticism and variety became fashionable; the picture opposite shows the thatched shell house at Jordans, near Ilminster, whose mixed architectural antecedents produce a building of fanciful charm.

The early part of the nineteenth century produced a great variety of summer houses which, since they were constructed of wood, have mostly disappeared. A typical structure of this period would be the rustic summer house shown above. There might also be Scottish cottages, 'as to architectural style, something between Gothic and Grecian'; Polish cottages (timber and wickerwork, with shingles on the roof); and Russian cottages built of solid logs.

Most charming were moss houses. Of rustic timber-work, they had slatted walls in which were packed as many species of moss as could be collected in the district. These were kept alive by judicious watering.

Arbours were constructed of odd materials. Roots and the bases of trunks might form the uprights, covered with a thatched roof. This root house at Spetchley Park in Worcestershire still stands.

The greater use of public parks resulted in summer houses—or shelters—on a grander scale. This fine building in the Italian style of about 1860 looks out on to the fountains in Kensington Gardens.

143

Temples of Love, favoured early in the present century, such as the one illustrated opposite now at Old Westbury on Long Island, seem to be descendants of the celebrated Temple of Love in the Trianon, inaugurated at a fête given by the Queen for the King in 1778. In the original was enclosed a symbolic statue of Love by Bouchardon.

Shown below is the early-twentieth-century, finely-wrought garden house in the classical manner at Luton Hoo, Bedfordshire. Clipped yew hedges at the corner of the formal garden, overshadowed by a weighty cedar, provide an effective setting.

During the first part of this century many pleasing summer houses were built in traditional local materials but of varying and ingenious design. A good example is that at Great Rissington Manor, Gloucestershire, illustrated here.

Even more original in conception, but using the elemental materials of stone, timber and thatch, is the summer house at Hascombe Court, Godalming (opposite), which stands by the rock-garden.

The inspiration of mountains

General interest in mountains, mountaineering and mountain plants is a comparatively modern phenomenon. It can be dated to such scientific works as von Haller's alpine flora in 1741 (he was also a poet, publishing *Die Alpen* in 1731, which is said to have gone through thirty editions in forty-five years) and de Saussure's *Voyages dans les Alpes*. Yet, centuries before that, caves, which to some extent may be associated with mountains, had strangely attracted man. In the sixteenth century, if not earlier, were made fanciful and sometimes richly decorated grottos (the name comes from the Greek for a vault).

It might be thought that mounts, those earthen piles which were features of medieval gardens, were ancestors of rock-gardens; but this does not seem to be so. It is possible that, like grottos, they may have had some symbolic meaning, but generally they are assumed to have been no more than vantage points from which to view the surrounding countryside over the high walls that usually enclosed early gardens.

There are three kinds of rock-gardening. The first is purely ornamental, and has resulted in some extraordinary constructions. The second aims to provide a close imitation of the geological formation of a fragment of mountain, in which are grown plants more or less natural to it. The third is solely concerned with the cultivation of plants from high mountains. This last was, in the late eighteenth century, probably the first sort of alpine gardening, and today, by the use of the alpine house, it has become a skilled branch of horticultural technique. But as it has no concern with art, it need not be discussed here.

Rock-gardening as a serious art may be said, with a fair amount of accuracy, to have begun during the years before the outbreak of war in 1914. Reginald Farrer (1880–1920) was the masterly spokesman of the new style. The rock-garden, he wrote, should be an entity on its own, away from the garden proper. It should take as its theme some particular mountain feature and reproduce it structurally. In its crevices, and spreading over its stones or appearing in its artificial screes, should grow the sort of plant that would be found naturally in such situations. A great deal of artistry and science could be, and often was, embodied in such a construction.

Conversely, Farrer and his school abhorred the 'dog's graveyard' style of rockery then in fashion, whose stones, often originating in builders' yards, were thrust in to give a spiky effect.

Something of the strange mixture of artifice and premature romanticism can be seen in this grotto at the Vatican gardens. Sometimes the mystic spirit of the grotto was even more confined within architectural forms.

In the eighteenth century grottos became much more sophisticated. The poet Alexander Pope made his the home of a collection of minerals which lined the walls. Genteel young ladies would spend hours patiently lining walls with shells, as can be seen in the illustration opposite of the Shell Grotto at St Giles House, Wimborne St Giles.

The first rock-gardens were rather strange and mainly concerned with rockwork (though sometimes old tree stumps were used). They remotely resembled Chinese pictures, and some were inspired by *chinoiserie*. One of the first was built by William Forsyth at the Chelsea Physic Gardens in 1774 with stones that came from the Tower of London, flints, chalk, and lava brought home by Sir Joseph Banks from his visit to Iceland. The rockery in the Liverpool Botanic Garden benefited from an assemblage of foreign rocks brought into the port as ship's ballast.

The type of structure in favour during the early part of the nineteenth century, is shown above. Here and there examples of this style may still be found, as at Chatsworth. They now have considerable charm, but are not acceptable to the modern alpine gardener.

Today, the enthusiast has no doubt travelled on foot, camera laden, about the Alps and even beyond. He has photographed primulas growing on the Bernina Pass (above) and on his return will try and recapture this mountain scene.

If he is not too much of a purist (and incidentally is an extremely skilful cultivator) he may grow successfully these mountain gems in an elegantly designed garden just under the window of his house, even if this be, as is Mr Roy Elliott's (shown below), only a couple of miles from the centre of Birmingham.

An entirely different type of rock-garden was that made by the late Mr F. J. Hanbury, who was both a distinguished botanist and gardener. Chance excavations showed that under what was apparently a meadow in his garden at Brockhurst, East Grinstead, there was an elaborate structure of rock. This was developed to make literally a rock garden (opposite) of both botanical and horticultural interest.

The joy of the alpine gardener is that within a few square yards he may encompass the plants not only of different continents but of the two hemispheres. He may enjoy the beauty of the unfolding leaves of an onion, *Allium karataviense* (below left) from Turkestan and the flowering of the choice New Zealand daisy, *Celmisia hieracifolia* (below right).

Another style of rock-garden is this one at Rushymead, Buckingham-shire. In it we have the rocks set naturally, as at the behest of Farrer, and a small pool carrying water-lilies, the margin planted with primulas and bog plants. (It should here be mentioned that bog gardens, not always logically, are often combined with alpine gardens.) The banks grow dwarf conifers—again (these are for the most part not natural plants but horticultural sports) and such sophisticated shrubs as wisteria and varieties of the Japanese maple. The whole, indeed, gives something of the effect of a Japanese gar-den. It is a charming and successful piece of design—yet, to the purist, coming under no special classification. It does, however, again remind one that Reginald Farrer in his early days visited Japan and was enthusiastic about the Japanese gardens.

We have already suggested that, perhaps more than in any other kind of gardening except that of the greenhouse, alpine gardening is now primarily for the plantsman—and one who delights in small plants. He can grow—again with little botanical logic—*Tulipa aucheriana* from the mountains of Persia (opposite), whose flowers almost outshine the sun on an early spring day.

Not far away, flowering rather later, may be that always exciting European alpine *Saxifraga longifolia*, in the form so aptly known as 'Tumbling Waters', and shown opposite.

In a shady spot there may also be this small woodlander, *Schizocodon soldanelloides illicifolium* (even Farrer complained about the name), which, like so many Japanese plants, has a curiously natural air of artifice, and artifice which accords well with much that is to be found in the art of gardens.

ACKNOWLEDGEMENTS

The author and publishers gratefully acknowledge the following who supplied photographs and permission to reproduce them. (References are to page numbers.)

Martyn Clémans 109–10

Coventry Evening Telegraph 65

Gerti Deutsch 4, 49–54, 111, 116

J. E. Downward 96

Roy Elliott 152–3, 155 (left and right), 157–9

The Frick Collection, New York 28

The Gardens of Japan by Jiro Harada, edited by Geoffrey Holme, The Studio, 1928 107–8, 112–14

Gottscho-Schleisner 102, 104–5

Government of India Regional Tourist Office 55–7

Miles Hadfield 58–60, 63, 74–5, 78, 82 (top and bottom), 83, 92–3, 100, 103, 132–4, 138, 142–3, 145

Iris Hardwick 88–9, 118, 136–7, 140

Peter Hunt 122, 125

A. J. Huxley 2, 38, 64, 86

Humphrey and Vera Joel 67, 77, 115, 123, 129, 147, 156

The late A. T. Johnson 127

W. T. Jones 37

A. F. Kersting 84–5, 87, 95, 97, 99, 120–1, 150

Longwood Gardens, Pennsylvania 72–3

Modern Gardens British and Foreign by Percy S. Crane, edited by Geoffrey Holme and Shirley B. Wainwright, The Studio, 1926–7 70, 76, 146, 154

Martin Nellist, National Institute of Agricultural Engineering 66

Old Westbury Gardens, Long Island 71, 124, 144

R. F. Pearson 35

Radio Times Hulton Picture Library 27

Rijksmuseum, Amsterdam 46

Edwin Smith 7, 9–25, 42–4, 47–8, 119, 128, 149

H. Smith 61

G. S. Thomas 32, 39, 62, 90, 94, 98, 101, 126, 130, 135

Virginia Chamber of Commerce 68–9, 139

Ian G. Walker Ltd 55–7